Brandywine River Museum

Chadds Ford, Pennsylvania

Millstones like those used at Hoffman's Mill are found
throughout the Museum's grounds.

A view from the Museum's courtyard provides a glimpse of the Brandywine Conservancy's
unique and extensive gardens.

On the banks of a historic stream in Chadds Ford, Pennsylvania,
a unique place for American art opened its doors in 1971. Incredibly, nearly 200,000 visitors
discovered the Brandywine River Museum that first year and toured its inaugural
exhibition, *The Brandywine Heritage*. Today, millions of visitors later, this 19th-century
grist mill that was converted into a 20th-century art museum has established a national
and international reputation for the quality of its collection and programs.

FROM MILL TO MUSEUM

Three galleries in the old mill building boast original structural beams, white plaster walls, and wide-board pine floors; the fourth, the Andrew Wyeth gallery, features flexible wall partitions and a revolutionary skylight system. All galleries open from a circular, brick-floored core — a symbolic silo for the old mill — with dramatic walls of glass, providing spectacular views of the Brandywine River and the rural landscape that inspired many of the artists represented in the museum's carefully focused collection.

Renowned works by N.C., Andrew, and James Wyeth and other artists from the Brandywine region hang near fascinating American still life paintings, important landscapes, and an unparalleled collection of American illustration. Instead of trying to replicate the encyclopedic collections of other museums, the Brandywine River Museum focuses its collection and exhibitions on American art of the 19th and 20th centuries and primarily art related to the heritage of its region.

PRESERVING AN AMERICAN HERITAGE

The story of how this museum came to be goes back many years and is intertwined with the historical and environmental concerns of the Brandywine Conservancy, the parent organization of the museum.

In the 1600s and 1700s, the Brandywine Valley was an agricultural and industrial center and site of Lenni Lenape Indian settlements. During the American Revolution, it was also a battlefield. Through-

Cover: N.C. Wyeth (1882-1945) *The Hunter*, ca. 1906. Oil on canvas, 38 7/8 x 26 5/8 in. Cover of *Outing Magazine*, June 1907.
Page 1: The Brandywine River, its surrounding landscape and its fascinating history have inspired generations of artists.
Page 2-3: Built in 1864 as a grist mill, Hoffman's Mill was renovated and opened in 1971 as the Brandywine River Museum.
Page 3 inset: Gracefully curved lobbies with glass walls provide panoramic views of the landscape beyond.

The wildflower and native plant gardens surrounding the Museum
provide a dramatic example of the use of native plants in public spaces.
Miss Gratz, a life-size bronze sculpture of a cow by Pennsylvania artist J. Clayton Bright,
is part of the Museum's sculpture collection.

out the 19th and early 20th centuries, agriculture and industry continued to coexist.

THE QUIET REVOLUTION

In the mid-1960s, the historic Brandywine Valley which had inspired artists through two centuries faced the threat of massive industrial development. The impact in floodplain areas, in particular, would have been devastating to the water supply for numerous communities in southeastern Pennsylvania and northern Delaware, including the city of Wilmington.

The protection of this water supply, and the surrounding open space and natural resources that sustain it, is the primary mission of the Conservancy's Environmental Management Center. Tens of thousands of acres of critical watershed land have been protected, in perpetuity, by conservation easements donated to the Brandywine Conservancy.

Appreciating the need for fast action, a group of local residents bought endangered land in Chadds Ford at auction and founded the Brandywine Conservancy in 1967. Soon thereafter, the newly-formed nonprofit organization purchased Hoffman's Mill—formerly a gristmill—on the banks of the Brandywine. In 1971 the Brandywine River Museum opened in the mill, which had been converted by architect James R. Grieves in harmony with the surrounding landscape and the region's history and art.

THE BRANDYWINE TRADITION

During much of the 19th century landscape painting was the dominant form of visual expression and many artists ventured to the Brandywine Valley, where they were captivated by the tranquility, history and architecture. By 1819, Bass Otis had published the nation's first lithograph—a Chester County scene entitled *House and Trees at Waterside*. Within a few decades well-known members of the Hudson River School, including Thomas Doughty, Edward Moran, and Jasper Cropsey, had documented the distinctive beauty of the region. Some, like William Trost Richards, chose to remain in the area and created powerful works here. Landscape painting has continued here throughout the 20th century and is represented in the canvases

Covered bridges that dot the Brandywine Valley landscape include two historic bridges
at the Brandywine Conservancy's nature preserve, the Laurels.
Pristine natural areas like the Laurels help to maintain the natural beauty of the Brandywine Valley
as well as its water quality and habitats.

of painters as diverse as Clifford Ashley, Peter Hurd, John McCoy, and George Weymouth.

STILL LIFE AND GENRE PAINTING

Still life painting also has strong roots in the Brandywine region, particularly *trompe l'oeil* or "fool the eye" painting that was popular in the late 19th century. The museum's collection includes several examples by such painters as William Michael Harnett, the acknowledged leader of this type of painting, John F. Peto, George Cope, and John Haberle. Many of these works were created for gentlemen's clubs, pubs, and other "masculine" interiors, hence the decidedly male subject matter—hunting and fishing equipment, dead game, mugs and pipes. The museum's collection includes works by other important American still life painters, including Raphael Peale, J. Alden Weir, and John F. Francis, who did not work in the trompe l'oeil style.

The related field of American genre painting of the 19th and 20th centuries is exemplified by interior scenes by Horace

Pippin and Jefferson David Chalfant, both of whom lived and worked in this river valley. These artists' works, along with many others frequently exhibited, are examples of the enormous artistic heritage of the Brandywine region.

ROOTS OF AMERICAN ILLUSTRATION

The heritage of the region—historical and visual—has many elements: landscapes, still lifes, genre paintings, and especially American illustration.

The first of the illustrators was the famous F.O.C. Darley, who left New York in 1859 to settle just north of Wilmington, Delaware. A few decades later, Howard Pyle, who is often termed "the Father of American Illustration," also came to work in the Brandywine Valley and set up an extraordinarily influential art school in Wilmington and Chadds Ford. He trained dozens of artists here, including N.C. Wyeth, Harvey Dunn, Jessie Willcox Smith, and Frank Schoonover — all of whom are represented in the Brandywine River Museum's collection, and many of

The architecture of the Brandywine River Museum artfully combines the old and the new, augmenting the 1864 mill structure with walls of glass.
Original wooden beams, wide-board floors and rough plaster walls in the galleries evoke the feeling of Hoffman's Mill.

whom worked in the region throughout their careers.

Successful illustration, Howard Pyle taught, should contain four elements: subject matter firmly rooted in history and personal experience; images that convey the artist's imagination, seriousness of purpose and commitment to craft; the choice of the right moment in the text; and dramatic use of light and of sharply contrasting values.

Thus American illustration is a central component of the museum's focused collection. Few, if any, museums in the world have such an important and extensive collection of this unique art form. Among the hundreds of illustrators represented in the museum's collection are early 20th-century giants, such as Maxfield Parrish, Edwin Austin Abbey, Howard Chandler Christy, Charles Dana Gibson, Rose O'Neill and Rockwell Kent; late 20th-century cartoonists, such as Al Hirschfeld, Charles Addams, and Edward Gorey; and contemporary illustrators, such as Charles Santore and Nancy Ekholm Burkert.

THREE GENERATIONS OF WYETH ART

N.C. Wyeth was profoundly moved by the Brandywine Valley when he arrived here to study with Howard Pyle in 1902. He wrote of the historic, rolling Brandywine countryside,

> "Never have I appreciated nature as I have in this place....this is a country full of restraints. Everything lies in its subtleties, everything is so gentle and simple, so unaffected."

He married, settled in Chadds Ford, raised a family, and within a decade had established himself among America's foremost illustrators, with his work featured in magazines and newspapers and in numerous very popular books.

N.C. Wyeth's five children inherited much talent. Daughters Henriette Wyeth Hurd and Carolyn Wyeth gained recognition as painters. Ann Wyeth McCoy, who painted during her youth, became a music composer. Eldest son, Nathaniel, was a widely respected chemist and inventor with the DuPont Company. Andrew

N.C. Wyeth, patriarch of the Wyeth family, came to Chadds Ford to study
with illustrator Howard Pyle.
Andrew Wyeth and his son James Wyeth continue
the family's artistic tradition.

Photo by Michael Ahearn

Wyeth, the youngest child of N.C., has become one of the most influential and best known painters in the history of American art. His masterful images in egg tempera and watercolor are often thought to be exact representations of scenes or people. Yet, in fact, Wyeth restructures elements of visible reality, arranging people and objects as he pleases, in order to create his private vision.

The third generation of the Wyeth family includes Andrew Wyeth's son, painter James Wyeth. By his early 20s, James Wyeth had garnered the national spotlight with a posthumous portrait of John F. Kennedy and other work, followed by striking portraits of Rudolf Nureyev and Andy Warhol. Since then, he has established his own style, characterized by strong images and sharp contrasts in his landscapes and portraits.

THE N.C. WYETH STUDIO

The Brandywine River Museum's collection and library contain some of N.C. Wyeth's finest works of art, as well as first edition publications and memorabilia documenting his life and contributions to American art history. This remarkable collection became unparalleled when the museum received gifts from the Wyeth family of N.C. Wyeth's house and studio and their contents. These buildings, together with the valuable artifacts they hold, are shared with the American public. Based on original photographs, drawings, paintings and letters, the studio has been restored as it was in 1945, at the time of N.C. Wyeth's death, and is now open for tours on a limited basis. Most of the artifacts on view there, including art, painting equipment, props and furniture, are original to the studio. As a result, visitors have a unique opportunity to see both Wyeth's art and the environment in which it was created.

A BRANDYWINE CHRISTMAS

The popular "Brandywine Christmas" exhibition is held annually between Thanksgiving and New Year's Day. Families return year after year to see the renowned display of operating O-gauge

N.C. Wyeth's studio, built in 1911 and expanded in 1923, is where the artist
created most of his famous works.
The studio has been restored as it was in 1945,
the year of N.C. Wyeth's death.

model trains and, every other year, Ann Wyeth McCoy's remarkable antique dolls. An exquisite Victorian dollhouse and beloved natural "critters, angels, and stars" ornaments crafted by museum volunteers also highlight the season. "A Brandywine Christmas" features changing exhibitions exploring topics such as images of Santa Claus in American illustration, illustrations for Grimm's fairy tales, and illustrations by James Wyeth for the children's book *The Stray*, written by Betsy James Wyeth.

NATIVE PLANT GARDENS

Surrounding the museum are stands of wildflowers, trees, and shrubs of the greater Brandywine region. The staff of the Brandywine Conservancy selects plants that provide a succession of bloom from early spring through the first frost, and each plant is located in a setting akin to its natural habitat: woodland, wetland, floodplain, or meadow. The naturalized gardens provide pleasure to visitors, serve as a valuable educational resource to horticulturalists, and give inspiration to gardeners who wish to use native plants in their own locations.

OUR MISSION

The Brandywine Conservancy and Brandywine River Museum were founded to "preserve, protect, interpret, utilize, and display American artistic, natural, and historical resources, principally of the Brandywine region, for the benefit of present and future generations." Throughout the year, the museum features a variety of changing exhibitions related to the art of the Brandywine Valley. Some of these exhibitions examine the career of one artist. Others examine a topic and feature works by several painters or illustrators. Still others feature decorative arts such as Amish and commemorative quilts, walking sticks, American silver, mocha ware, decorative tiles, and even carousel carvings. Through the museum's collection and exhibitions, the N.C. Wyeth studio, and the Conservancy's native plant gardens, visitors' experiences are at once entertaining, educational, and enlightening.

THOMAS DOUGHTY (1793–1856)

Gilpin's Mill on the Brandywine, 1830
Oil on canvas, 7 1/4 x 11 in.

Doughty was one of the earliest American painters to devote himself exclusively
to landscape painting. A forerunner of Thomas Cole and the Hudson River School
of landscape painting, Doughty's works evoke picturesque nature,
and have only a hint of natural drama.

WILLIAM TROST RICHARDS (1833–1905)

The Valley of the Brandywine, Chester County (September), 1886-1887
Oil on canvas, 40 x 55 in.

William Trost Richards is one of the best-known and most important 19th-century
American landscape painters. He purchased a Chester County farm in 1884
and there produced a number of fine landscapes, including the large canvas,
The Valley of the Brandywine, Chester County.

JASPER CROPSEY (1823–1900)

Autumn on the Brandywine River, 1887
Oil on canvas, 10 3/4 x 20 1/2 in.

Initially trained as an architect, Cropsey decided to become a painter in 1841.
After seven years in Europe, he returned to paint mainly autumnal scenes. His work reveals
the strong influence of both Thomas Cole and Asher B. Durand.
He is regarded as a second-generation Hudson River School painter.

JOHN HABERLE (1856–1933)

Torn in Transit, 1890–1895
Oil on canvas, 13 1/2 x 17 in.

Although best known as a trompe l'oeil still-life painter, early in his career Haberle painted
more "serious" subjects, including landscapes and fruit still lifes.
His decision to incorporate a landscape scene in this tromp l'oeil painting, one of a series
of works depicting "images within images," may have been a nostalgic return to the themes
of his earlier career and a reaction to his encroaching blindness.

WILLIAM MICHAEL HARNETT (1848–1892)

A Man's Table Reversed, 1877
Oil on canvas, 12 x 10 1/4 in.

Still lifes of newspapers, mugs, pipes, fruit, dead game, hunting rifles,
and other familiar objects were extremely popular with a public that loved seeing ordinary objects
of their world depicted. In this painting, Harnett has achieved an artful arrangement that
harmoniously balances simple, common, even mundane objects.

GEORGE COPE (1855–1929)

The Hunter's Equipment (The Hunter's Yellow Jacket), 1891
Oil on canvas, 52 x 32 in.

Cope, who hailed from nearby West Chester, Pennsylvania,
turned to trompe l'oeil painting about 1891. Cope was especially drawn to hunting subjects,
a preference that may have been affected by such works as *After the Hunt*, which
William Michael Harnett, leader of the trompe l'oeil movement, painted in 1885.

JEFFERSON DAVID CHALFANT (1856–1931)

Envious Critics, 1894
Oil on board, 8 1/2 x 12 5/8 in.

Chalfant, who began his career painting trompe l'oeil still-lifes
in the style of William Michael Harnett, switched to genre subjects, especially children and artisans,
in the early 1890s. *Envious Critics* is a fine example of these, presenting an anecdotal scene
of his subjects' lives, interests, and relationships, and avoids sentimentality.

HORACE PIPPIN (1888–1946)

Saying Prayers, 1943
Oil on canvas, 16 x 20 1/8 in.

A major 20th-century primitive painter, Horace Pippin created images
of African American life, historical and biblical subjects, and still lifes that are an eloquent
testament to a talent that overcame obstacles of poverty, lack of instruction, and physical disability.
The simplicity of Pippin's technique allowed him to convey emotion in a direct,
effective manner, and thoroughly modern style.

HOWARD PYLE (1853–1911)

Frontispiece for *The Wonder Clock, or, Four and Twenty Marvelous Tales,*
Being One for Each Hour of the Day
(New York: Harper & Brothers, ca. 1888)
Ink on paper, 9 1/4 x 6 1/2 in.

Howard Pyle was a gifted writer as well as a celebrated illustrator, and even his children's books,
including *The Wonder Clock*, won acclaim for the integration of text, illustration, and book design.
It was these qualities that he taught his students to incorporate into their work.

HOWARD PYLE (1853–1911)

The Nation Makers, 1903
Oil on canvas, 40 1/4 x 26 in.

The Nation Makers, one of Pyle's finest works, is an excellent example
of the artist's interest in historical subjects, particularly themes of the Revolutionary War.
The painting conveys Pyle's response to the historical Brandywine battlefield,
which was close to where he lived and conducted many of his classes.

The Ox Driver, an Old Time Figure of the West, 1909
Oil on canvas, 34 7/8 x 26 in.
Frontispiece for *Century*, October 1909

Harvey Dunn trained at the South Dakota Agricultural School, the Art Institute of Chicago,
and Howard Pyle's School of Art in Wilmington, Delaware.
He became famous as an illustrator, war artist, painter of the West, and teacher.

FRANK SCHOONOVER (1877–1972)

Canadian Trapper (White Fang and Gray Beaver in Canoe), 1906
Oil on canvas, 35 3/8 x 19 5/8 in.
Illustration for Jack London's "White Fang," *Outing Magazine*, July 1906

Schoonover, who studied with Howard Pyle at the same time N.C. Wyeth did,
earned a reputation as a painter of the Canadian wilderness. Like Wyeth, he traveled extensively.
His first-hand experience with Eskimo fur traders provided inspiration for many years.

The Russians at the Gate of Herat, 1885
Ink on paper, 8 5/8 x 9 3/8 in.

Thomas Nast launched his career as a cartoonist during the 1864 presidential elections.
Among his enduring images are the Republican elephant, Democratic donkey, and Tammany tiger.
The Russians at the Gate of Herat is a commentary on the British policy of non-involvement
in the on-going Russo-Turkish War.

CHARLES DANA GIBSON (1867–1944)

The Education of Mr. Pipp: Mr. Pipp Meets Two of the Courier's Intimate Friends,
a Prince and a Duke, 1898
Ink on paper, 19 3/8 x 28 3/8 in.

One of the most famous American illustrators of the late 19th century,
Gibson focused on elements of style and elegance in society. For the Mr. Pipp series, however,
he added well-honed satirical humor.

JESSIE WILLCOX SMITH (1863–1935)

Goldilocks and the Three Bowls, ca. 1900
Mixed media on board, 21 1/2 x 14 3/4 in.

A student of Howard Pyle at Drexel Institute who also studied at the
Pennsylvania Academy of the Fine Arts, Jessie Willcox Smith came to the field of illustration
after working several years as a kindergarten teacher in the early 1880s.
She gained wide popularity for her illustrations of children.

I Do Not Know the Answer to that Riddle, 1907
Mixed media on paper, 14 1/4 x 10 1/4 in.
Illustration for Frances Hodgson Burnett, "The Cozy Lion," *St. Nicholas*, February 1907

After working as a free-lance illustrator, Cady began a seventeen year association
with the first *Life Magazine*, creating numerous satirical drawings.

FREDERIC REMINGTON (1861–1904)

The Canadian Mounted Police on a "Musical Ride" — "Charge," 1887
Oil on board, 15 1/4 x 23 1/2 in.

New York-born Frederic Remington was a noted sculptor, painter, illustrator, and writer.
After a year at Yale University he went to the West, where his experiences
as a cowboy and accompanying military troops in Indian campaigns
gave inspiration to his life's work.

N.C. WYETH (1882–1945)

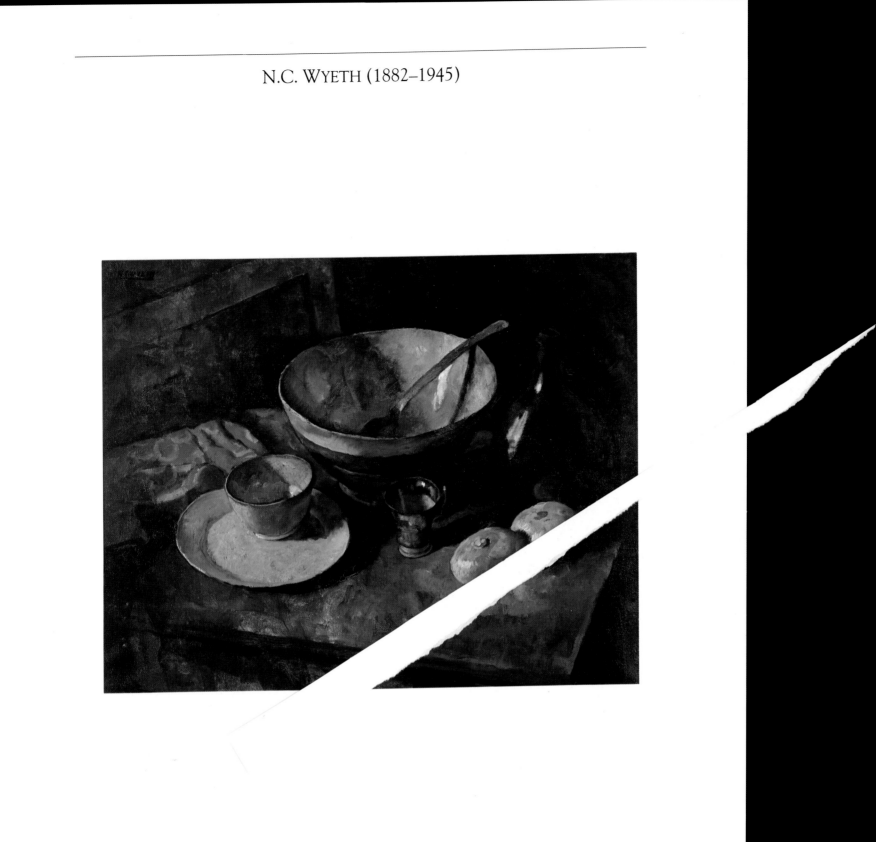

Still Life with Onions, ca. 1924
Oil on canvas, 32 1/4 x 47 1/4 in.

N.C. Wyeth drew inspiration from many sources when he painted still lifes in the 1920s and 30s.
This canvas displays his brilliant ability to transform the ordinary into the extraordinary.

N.C. WYETH (1882–1945)

In the Crystal Depths, 1906
Oil on canvas, 38 x 26 in.
Illustration for *Outing Magazine*, June 1907

This painting was one in a set of five. N.C. Wyeth was a student of Native American customs
and culture, and his admiration is abundantly apparent in the care he took
in depicting the canoe and figure of this introspective, woodland Indian.

N.C. WYETH (1882–1945)

The Fight in the Forest, 1919
Oil on canvas, 40 1/2 x 32 1/4 in.
Illustration for *The Last of the Mohicans: A Narrative of 1757* by James Fenimore Cooper
(New York: Charles Scribner's Sons, 1919)

After Wyeth's illustrations for *Treasure Island* appeared in 1911,
he won commissions to illustrate many more books, including *Kidnapped* (1913), *The Black Arrow* (1916),
The Boy's King Arthur (1917), *Robin Hood* (1917), *The Mysterious Island* (1918), *The Last of the Mohicans* (1919),
Westward Ho (1920), *The Scottish Chiefs* (1921), *The White Company* (1922), *David Balfour* (1924),
and *The Deerslayer* (1925).

N.C. WYETH (1882–1945)

Jim Hawkins Leaves Home, 1911
Oil on canvas, 47 1/4 x 36 1/8 in.
Illustration for Robert Louis Stevenson's *Treasure Island*
(New York: Charles Scribner's Sons, 1911)

With an acute sense of the role of skillful illustration to advance the narrative,
N.C. Wyeth chose a minor episode in the text of *Treasure Island*.
His contrast between stark light and deep shadow, a technique Wyeth learned from Howard Pyle,
heightened the tension and alludes to the danger Hawkins will face.

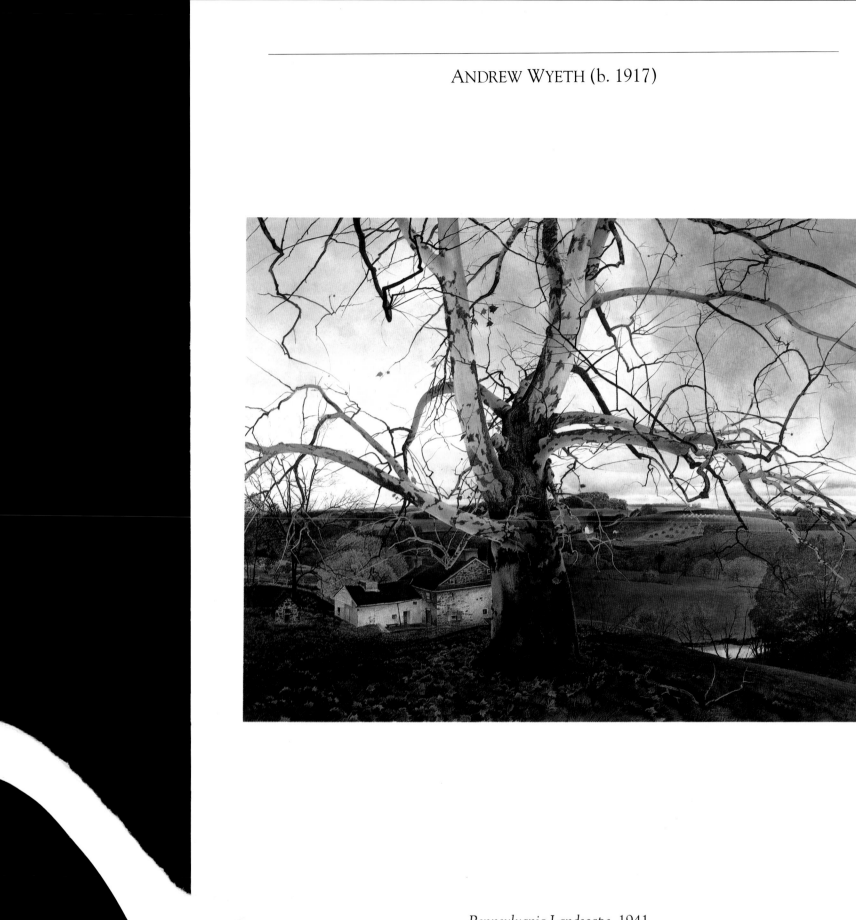

Pennsylvania Landscape, 1941
Tempera on panel, 35 1/4 x 47 1/8 in.

The limited subject matter, media, and colors suggest an artist deliberately restraining himself,
refusing to allow technical flamboyance or self-indulgence to overwhelm emotion and ideas.
This image is a composite of many scenes in various parts of Chadds Ford.

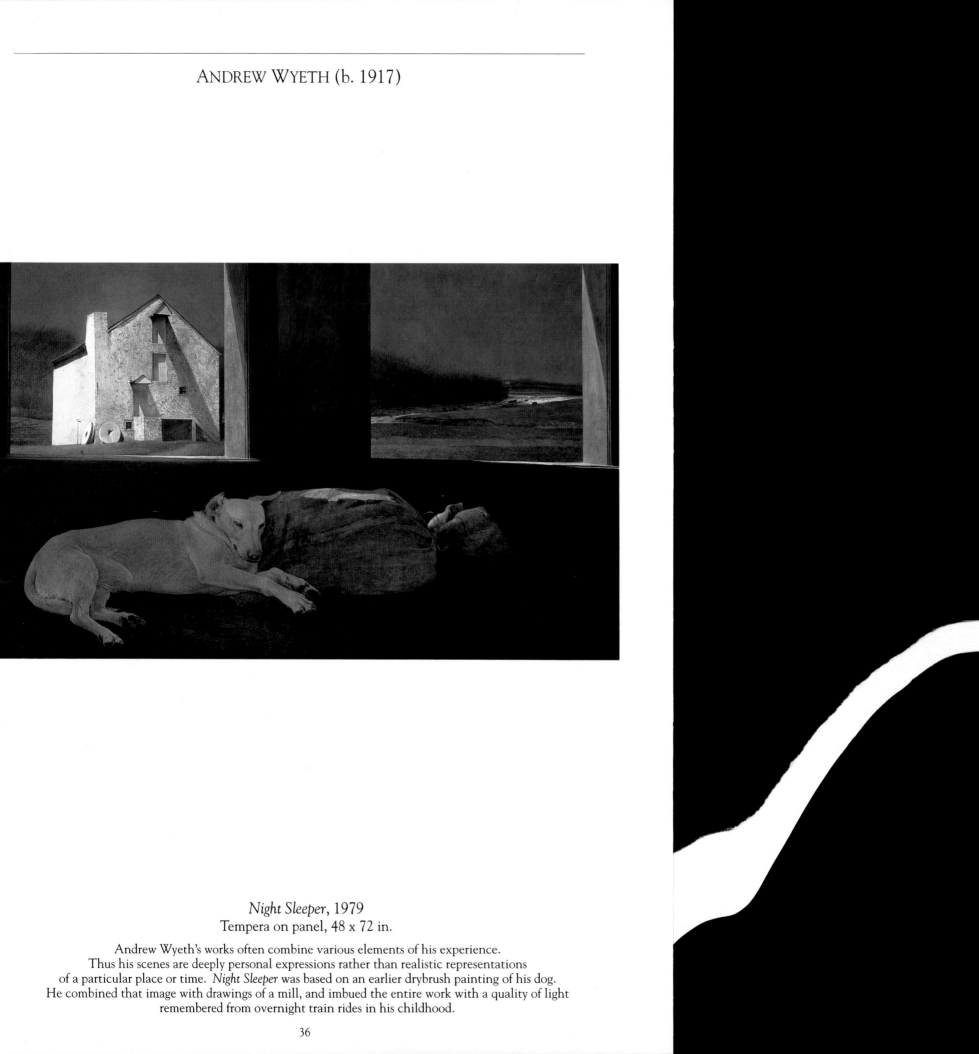

Night Sleeper, 1979
Tempera on panel, 48 x 72 in.

Andrew Wyeth's works often combine various elements of his experience.
Thus his scenes are deeply personal expressions rather than realistic representations
of a particular place or time. *Night Sleeper* was based on an earlier drybrush painting of his dog.
He combined that image with drawings of a mill, and imbued the entire work with a quality of light
remembered from overnight train rides in his childhood.

36

ANDREW WYETH (b. 1917)

Roasted Chestnuts, 1956
Tempera on panel, 48 x 33 in.

Roasted Chestnuts expresses more than the isolation and loneliness
often suggested in Wyeth's paintings. A rutted road reaching to a distant horizon is a recurrent theme
in his work. In this case, the solitary yet determined youth looking toward the lighted horizon
expresses a patient acceptance of fate.

ANDREW WYETH (b. 1917)

Monologue, 1965
Dry brush watercolor on paper, 22 1/4 x 28 1/2 in.

Monologue, so named because William Snowden chatted incessantly during each sitting,
exemplifies Wyeth's dry brush technique. Dry brush allows an artist to include
much greater detail than would watercolor alone.

CAROLYN WYETH (1909–1994)

Open Window, 1944
Oil on canvas, 25 x 36 in.

Carolyn Wyeth's love of quiet and solitude infused all of her works
with a sensuous aura. The wine-red flower, heavy gray curtains, and clear sky simultaneously
convey past sorrow and future hope. The stark geometry and strong coloration of the composition
contrast with the subtle romantic atmosphere and image.

PETER HURD (1904–1984)

A Summer Evening, 1968
Tempera on panel, 23 x 25 15/16 in.

Although he worked in oils when he studied with N.C. Wyeth,
Peter Hurd taught himself the techniques of egg tempera and introduced the medium to both
N.C. and Andrew Wyeth. In *A Summer Evening*, Hurd expresses the texture of the scoured hills,
dry, brittle grassland, and windswept trees.

JAMES WYETH (b. 1946)

Giuliana and the Sunflowers, 1987
Oil on board, 16 1/2 x 20 1/2 in.

James Wyeth trained with his aunt Carolyn; however, some of his techniques
suggest the influence of his father and grandfather. His paintings possess strong central images
and sharp contrasts, as did most of his grandfather's work.
His paintings often show a somber side, as do his father's.

JAMES WYETH (b. 1946)

Wolfbane, 1984
Mixed media on paper, 28 1/4 x 22 in.

Wolfbane is a portrait of the artist's wife. The focus is on her hat and her scarf
which is wound about a floral sprig. Dramatic lighting within the rich dark background
defines and even animates the hat and chair,
imparting a sense of mystery to the setting.

GEORGE A. WEYMOUTH (b. 1936)

August, 1974
Tempera on panel, 48 x 48 in.

George A. Weymouth has long been interested in realism,
and his distinctive style is highly regarded. Andrew Wyeth and Peter Hurd suggested
he try painting with egg tempera and he uses it and watercolor
for portraits as well as landscapes.

Antique dolls from the collection of Ann Wyeth McCoy are often exhibited as part of *A Brandywine Christmas*, the Museum's annual holiday display.

O-gauge model trains are an annual feature of *A Brandywine Christmas*, to the delight of many visitors.

Annual Events
Some of the most popular annual events in the region are held at the Brandywine River Museum. Many, like "A Brandywine Christmas," have taken their place in the traditions of many families. The Museum also has changing special exhibitions year round.

Wildflower, Native Plant and Seed Sale
Mother's Day Weekend
The Brandywine Conservancy's garden volunteers host an annual sale to benefit the Wildflower and Native Plant Gardens at the Conservancy.

Radnor Hunt Steeplechase Races
May
An afternoon of steeplechase
"Racing for Open Space" benefits the Conservancy's environmental programs. Races are held at the Radnor Hunt Club in Malvern, PA.

Annual Antiques Show
Memorial Day Weekend
The Museum volunteers host the annual Antiques Show, featuring dozens of major dealers, to benefit the Museum Volunteers' Purchase Fund acquiring art for the Brandywine River Museum's collection.

A Brandywine Christmas
Thanksgiving Weekend through early January
This annual holiday display offers such features as seasonal art and children's book illustrations, fine antique dolls, gold-and-gemstone jewelry and a large, rare Victorian dollhouse. Annual highlights include O-gauge model trains in an expansive layout and the renowned "Critters, Angels and Stars," natural ornaments displayed on trees and in settings throughout the Museum.

Brandywine River Museum
U.S. Route 1, Chadds Ford, PA 19317
610-388-2700

The Brandywine River Museum is accredited by the American Association of Museums and operated by the Brandywine Conservancy, Inc.

Museum Hours
Daily, 9:30 a.m. to 4:30 p.m.
Closed Christmas Day

Access for People with Disabilities
Available through the office entrance on the river side of the Museum. Special parking is available in the parking lot near the river.

Museum Shop
Open during regular Museum hours
Member's discount: 10% on regular purchase

Restaurant
Open daily for lunch

Credits:

Copyright © 1997 by the Brandywine River Museum of the Brandywine Conservancy, Inc.

All rights reserved

This book, or portions thereof, may not be reproduced in whole or in part in any form without the written permission of the Brandywine River Museum of the Brandywine Conservancy, Inc.

Text by Lucinda C. Laird

Text edited by Catherine E. Hutchins

Art photography by Rick Echelmeyer

Museum and exterior photography by Michael Kahn

Edited by James B. Patrick

Designed by Donald G. Paulhus

Printed in Hong Kong

Produced by Fort Church Publishers, Inc.
Little Compton, R.I. 02837

Published and distributed by the Brandywine River Museum, P.O. Box 141, Chadds Ford, PA 19317